No Matter the Question

MEDITATION

is the Answer

Becca Pronchick

ISBN: 978-1-941142-27-1

Edited by: Davina Rubin
www.davinarubin.com

Photographs Copyright © 2014 Becca Pronchick

Published by:
Becca Pronchick, CPCC
920 Foxboro Drive
Napa, CA 94559
707-253-8733

Email: bp@beccapronchick.com

www.permissiontorelax.com

ACKNOWLEDGEMENTS

This book is dedicated to all of the students who bring their light, love, and laughter into my meditation classes and retreats. You inspire me always.

My heartfelt thanks to Davina Rubin, my editor and friend, for her expertise, support, and abiding friendship. And a big thank you to Chris and Debbie O'Byrne at JETLAUNCH for their expertise and patience in publishing.

With unmeasurable gratitude to my teachers. I am honored and delighted by your stories, your wisdom, your generosity, and especially your love and encouragement for me to teach as well.

For my beloved husband, Steve, for his steady presence in my life with so much unconditional love, patience, dedication, and especially humor. You are the love of my life. And for my dear family, friends, and fellow travelers on the spiritual path. Thank you for sharing your light and love with me.

TABLE OF CONTENTS

PART ONE
IN THE BEGINNING

*I*f you are reading this book, you are probably curious about learning to meditate, or feel that meditation may be of benefit to you in some way. This is good—curiosity is a great place to start. Know that once you begin, you will never stop learning, which is part of the fun. This information may not answer each and every question that comes up in your life, however, you will have a place to turn for guidance, clarity, courage and connecting with your intuition and divine guidance, which will be a terrific source of support, no matter what challenges you face.

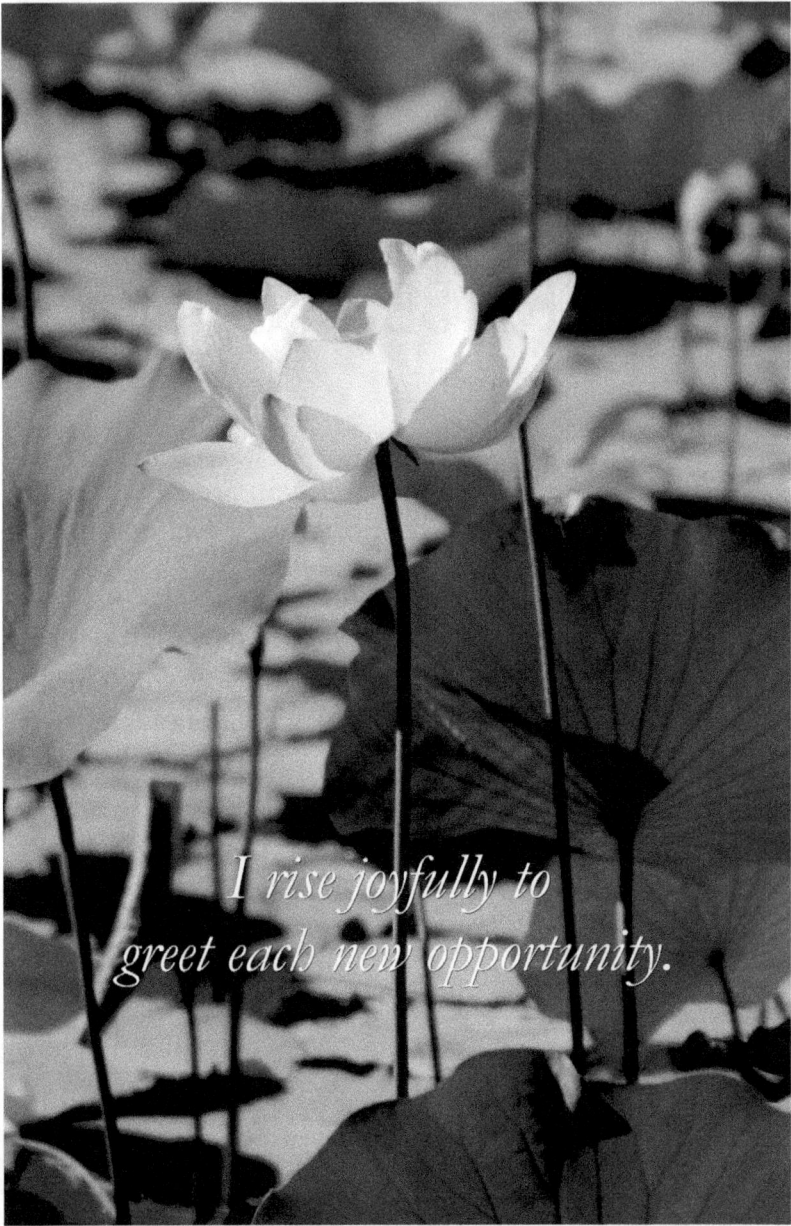

I rise joyfully to
greet each new opportunity.

INTRODUCTION
MY STORY SO FAR

*A*s I begin writing this book, my inner critic is shouting, "Who do you think you are, writing a book about meditation? An expert?"

Well, no. I think of myself as a meditator and a teacher, certainly not an expert. But it is exactly for that reason—that I am someone who has been meditating for a long time, who has experienced the highs and lows of meditation practice, and is aware of so many of the difficulties and discoveries that come with the inner journey of meditation—that I am writing this book in the hope that it will be a help to those who are beginning the journey.

As a teacher, I would like to pass on what I know, including how to deal with that "inner critic"—the one who would like nothing more than to keep us from meditating, so we don't learn how to put that critic outside and shut the door. And maybe this book will help some who have tried to meditate, maybe given up and tried again, and given up because they had the thought, "I'm just not good at this." I've been through all that, and I know the road, so I'm writing this book to help people to navigate the path of meditation.

To give you an idea of the journey, which brought me to meditation, a bit of background. I was raised in the Episcopal church in southern California, with the usual "go to church on Sundays and take the kids to Sunday school" type parents. My mother was raised as a Christian Scientist, but it was my grandmother, Leah, who deeply influenced me by teaching me—in a spiritual, rather than religious sense—the Golden Rule: "Do unto others as you would have them do unto you" or, "Treat others as you would like to be treated."

As a child I loved the ritual, the candles, the music and the flow of the seasons in the church. But as a teenager I became disenchanted with the church, and I stayed away from organized religion until, in my early thirties, I became involved in the Al-Anon twelve step recovery groups. I was introduced to the concept of a Higher Power, which felt good and comforting to me, and very different from the childhood image I had of a God with a beard and lightning bolt sitting on a throne in the clouds.

When I was a teenager in the 1960's I used to watch "Lilias Yoga & You" on television, which was my first experience of being a yoga student. Then in my 30's I took a beginning meditation class with a burning desire to calm down my chronic anxiety and Type A personality traits. I soon learned that there is so much more to meditation practice than sitting still or staring at a candle!

What I was hoping for, driven by, was the desire to heal my compulsive behavior and propensity to push myself unmercifully. I was hard on myself always, which is why I encourage being gentle with yourself—it's much more effective. The benefits of a daily meditation practice have gradually relieved my constant pushing, and have helped me to slow down the pace of my life. I am now able to listen within, to open to Divine guidance and my inner wisdom and intuition.

I want to make it clear that it wasn't always easy to stick with the practice. The concept of Daily Practice took me a long time to fully comprehend. In the early 1980's when I began, my meditation was "off and on"—more "off" than "on" would be accurate. Since the 1990's it has been mostly "on" because I have found that the more regular my meditation, the better my life. I find it to be of great benefit to my sanity, my concentration and my overall well-being.

I also learned that taking a class and having a dedicated group to practice with really helped me to deepen and anchor myself in the work. Finding a routine that works well for you takes dedication, persistence, patience and the support of others on the path. The rewards are profound and life-changing.

When I began to meditate and open up to my own personal concept of a Higher Power, I experienced a feminine presence that I later came to know as the Divine Mother or Goddess, whose primary characteristics are compassion and loving kindness. She is an enlightened being who has chosen to manifest in various forms on Earth to help all beings. I have a warm and wonderful relationship with the Divine Mother in the form of Quan Yin, the goddess of compassion.

When I was in my forties, I deepened my practice when I enrolled at The Expanding Light at Ananda in Nevada City for Yoga teacher training. Then I entered a 28-day residential training at Expanding Light, where we studied and practiced yoga and meditation morning, noon and night. I emerged with a strong daily practice and began to teach yoga and meditation in Napa.

Not long after my training at Ananda I was blessed to find a wonderful teacher, Julie Henderson, Ph.D., a somatic psychologist and Buddhist teacher. She has been instrumental in my growth and development as a practitioner and teacher. Sally Kempton, a teacher of Buddhist meditation for decades, has also been an important and loving presence in my journey to deepen my meditation practice.

I am living proof that no matter what one's background, religious or spiritual training, anyone will benefit from meditation. It has given me such a strong foundation for staying connected with myself, with my source and with all of life, and I am truly grateful to be sharing these gifts with you, dear students and friends.

BEFORE YOU BEGIN

I wish I had a nickel for every time someone has said to me, "I can't meditate!" The fact is, everyone has the ability to meditate, given some practice, a few simple techniques and the willingness to give it a go. But there are all sorts of things that come up when you begin which can stop you, make you feel you just can't do it.

When I initially was learning to meditate in my early thirties, I thought everyone but me could sit down, close their eyes and drop right into a place of peace and comfort. Ha! That certainly wasn't my experience. Ask anyone who has begun this journey, and they'll laugh and tell similar stories.

I took a meditation class where we were taught to gaze at a candle flame. I don't remember anything else about the class, except that I sat through class thinking, planning, fidgeting and wondering. But not meditating.

I took more classes, learned a bit more, and continued to practice. Down the road I read books about meditation, joined a meditation group—which I highly recommend.

Ultimately I trained as an Ananda yoga and meditation instructor. I am still studying, reading, taking classes and practicing nearly every day. Now I feel a bit off when I don't meditate.

So, having been through a portion of the journey myself, I want to share with you some things to be aware of before you start. When you see them happening, just know that you are on the right track, and that this is what happens to many, many people when they begin to take the first steps to control the mind through meditation.

SOME COMMON
OBSTACLES TO MEDITATION
(Moving Through the Obstacles to Meditation)

1. Feeling you don't want to meditate. "I just can't do this!" When you begin to meditate, you might have hidden standards about what you're supposed to do. Some think meditation has to be for 30 minutes to an hour for it to count. If you think that, you might be setting too high a bar for yourself, and get discouraged. This could make you feel that you don't want to meditate.

The best thing to do is to begin with very short meditations—even one minute—to get yourself started. Try to set aside time each day—even a minute or two—to meditate. The more you meditate routinely, even for a few minutes, the more you will want to turn within and quiet your mind, and unplug from your external activity. When you have developed a new habit of meditating every day, you will begin to see the benefits of focus, clarity, calm and peace within. The key is consistency. Try to do it every day; if you miss a day, don't get discouraged—just make sure you get back on track.

2. Restlessness. Until we begin, we don't realize that sitting still actually makes a tremendous demand on the body and mind. Most of the time our bodies are in motion and we hardly notice it. So once we stop moving, it can be very hard to maintain stillness. Allow for the fact that it takes time, each and every time you meditate, to go from movement to stillness, from outwardness to inwardness. This is true at every level of our being. Every moment of our lives we are active, unless we are asleep, and even then there is a certain level of movement of body and mind.

Meditation is being, not doing. Think of a lake, tumultuous on the surface, but still and calm at the depths. To get to the depths, you have to dive through the restless surface. This turbulence is so often with us every time we attempt to go within, especially at the start of things. So allow yourself time to get comfortable, to scratch and wiggle; then gently and firmly insist on physical stillness.

3. Physical Discomfort. Being physically comfortable is a very important aspect of meditation practice. The minute we sit down, determined to be still, all sorts of tiny (and not so tiny) aches, pains and annoyances crop up. It's as if our body is rebelling against us. One piece of advice is to observe the area of discomfort, note that it's there, but continue to sit. You will find that eventually it will fade into the background.

Exercise always helps. Stretching, or a few yoga postures before you begin to meditate will help greatly. To support your upright posture you can use pillows, pads, benches, a chair or whatever. Find a position that your body can maintain comfortably and still have the spine upright. Realize that your body will go through all sorts of discomforts to distract you; continue to maintain your stillness as best you can.

When I say that discomfort can be a distraction, I speak from experience. Several years ago I developed severe degenerative disc disease, and for over a year I was unable to sit for any length of time without considerable pain. I could, however, stand or lie down with some degree of comfort. During this period I was able to meditate lying down, or only slightly elevated on a pillow. Because my daily meditation practice was now a way of life, I found I could stay awake and effectively meditate, although I was horizontal. It might seem that meditation during that time might have felt a chore, given that I was in pain. But in fact, meditation was a great gift; recognizing that the body is not the only part of me gave me added insight and strength, and was probably part of my healing process. Now that my back is mostly healed, I am able once again, to meditate sitting up for some time.

4. No time to meditate. This is a very big snare. When you are short on time, the first tendency is to want to skip meditation. But the best thing to do in such a circumstance is to decrease the length of meditation, rather than skipping it altogether. Remember that you are working to develop a routine. Keep your meditation practice in place; go for quality rather than quantity, remembering that consistency is one of the most important aspects of a meditation practice. Even if you take five dedicated minutes to meditate on a rushed day, you are keeping your practice intact.

It also helps to learn to manage your time a little bit more wisely. Remember that if you meditate, your energy and concentration powers grow and you will use all of your time more efficiently. Experiment with the best time of day to meditate—first thing in the morning works best for me, but for others, the time when you get home after work might be best for releasing the day and having some quiet time before your evening meal. It's possible that before you go to sleep will be the best time for you, to let go of the day just past, give thanks, and spend a few minutes in silent contemplation to set the tone for your time of rest. Yogananda taught that we can enter sleep with an intention to rest well, rather than processing the activities of the day, and receive healing and learning during our sleep and dreams.

5. "I'm just not a good meditator!" This is a very insidious thought that may cause you to stop meditating entirely. And the fact is, it just isn't true! Meditation is a building experience. Each day we lay the foundation for a lifetime of meditation work. Some days are good, some days more difficult. You cannot measure your success as a meditator by judging a particular meditation, or even a series of meditations.

What is "a good meditation" anyway? St. Teresa of Avila said, "A meditation is well done if all you did was fight distraction. " The whole purpose of meditation techniques is to bring the mind back from being distracted. Note: I did not say, "to eliminate distraction." If you think once we have a meditation technique we should never be distracted, think again. Remember that the point of using meditation practices is to have something for the mind to return to. This is practicing meditation correctly. Each time you realize that you are distracted, calmly return to your technique. No matter how many times this happens during a meditation, calmly return and never give in to discouragement. Set your intention to never give up.

To help yourself stay on track, you can do a little check at the end of each day, and look at your life. Notice the subtle changes in your thinking, your behavior, and your reactions to challenges. This is the best way to measure the success of your meditation practice. Keep track of these, and you will see changes.

6. "I need to get a few things done before I start, so I have a clear path." Your habit may be to wait until all of the outside circumstances are lined up before you give yourself permission to relax and listen within. "I need to get all my e-mails caught up, then I'll start." "I'm going to start meditating when I'm done with my Spanish class." The fact is that a "to do" list never ends, and completing your "to do" list will happen with greater ease and clarity when you begin to practice meditation techniques every day, if only for a few minutes. You will discover what great relief, benefit and efficiency may be attained through meditation. Don't put it off—begin!

THE BENEFITS OF MEDITATION

- Calming the mind
- Increasing mental focus
- Gaining clarity
- Reducing mental anxiety
- Appreciating Silence
- Improving health and well-being
- Relieving stress
- Opening to Divine guidance
- Deepening connection with Self
- Physical and emotional healing
- Appreciating silence and stillness
- More restful than sleep

SIMPLE SUGGESTIONS TO GET YOU STARTED

- Set an intention to practice a little bit each day, if only for a few minutes.

- Incorporate meditation into your daily routine. Make it part of your day, just like brushing your teeth or taking a shower.

- Judge your practice not by the length of your meditation, but by how much better you feel as you move through your day. Note: This refers to how conscious and aware you are, and how you meet challenges.

You might also consider:

- Joining a meditation group in your area

- Purchasing and listening to a guided meditation CD to support you in your practice.

- Agreeing to meet with a friend or meditation partner regularly, to practice together. You can enjoy the combined energy and support.

PREPARING FOR MEDITATION

"The most important principle to understand about meditation is this: we meditate to know ourselves. We usually think of meditation as a practice or a process, yet meditation is also a relationship. If it is a process, then it is the process of coming into loving relationship with our own Consciousness."

Sally Kempton author of *Meditation for the Love of It*

*B*efore you actually move into meditation, settle yourself down; move mindfully through whatever steps feel comfortable to you, so that you become more relaxed. These steps might be taking a brief walk, or listening to soothing music. Find whatever works well for you to help you be settled in the present moment. Whatever technique you choose, it should help you to quiet your mind, and bring you into a receptive space. Allow some quiet time to rest in the silence. These techniques are useful in quieting your mind, getting you into a receptive state, so that you are ready to begin meditating.

Basic Technique—Focusing on the Breath

1. Sit comfortably with eyes closed and observe the breath moving in and out of the body.

2. Notice any sounds you hear—listen. When your mind wanders—gently begin again.

3. Observe the quality of the breath, the feeling of the air moving through your nostrils. Continue.

This may seem like a very simple practice. It is. It is also quite profound. Can you stay fully present and concentrate in this moment? Can you fully experience this breath without judgment or tension? Can you release the habit of telling a story about everything as it is happening? Be kind to yourself; cultivate happiness and contentment in this precious moment.

Breathe!

BEGINNING TO MEDITATE

*A*llow some quiet time to rest in the silence and listen with your heart.

1. Settle yourself down in a comfortable position, where you will not be disturbed for at least ten to twenty minutes. Find your comfortable seated position, whether in a chair or on your meditation cushion or bench on the floor. Shorter meditation periods are beneficial; even just a few minutes can be helpful. However, taking a bit more time for your mind and body to settle will give you great relief from stress, worry and fatigue, and energize you.

2. Sit so that your spine is long and open, supporting yourself with cushions if necessary. Allow the breath and energy to flow freely through your body. Find the most comfortable position for your body with your arms and legs relaxed.

3. Now begin to observe your breath—noticing the sensations of the breath in the nostrils or the rising and falling of the chest or abdomen. When your attention wanders, gently return your attention to the breath. The act of beginning again is the essential art of meditation practice—continue to be aware of your breath.

"You don't need to make the breath special. It doesn't have to be deep or long or different from however it is and however it changes. It's happening anyway, so simply be aware of it ... one breath at a time."

Insight Meditation Workbook
by Sharon Salzberg and Joseph Goldstein

4. Allow your awareness to settle down into your body. Notice any tension in your body or restless thoughts. Don't try to control the breath; just relax even more and allow your awareness to rest in just this breath— just this moment. Focus on the sensations of the breath, wherever you feel them moving—in your belly, your nostrils or your throat. At first your breathing may be deep. Eventually, as you allow your body to breathe, it will be more relaxed and slowed down. Your mind will follow your breath, quieting the thoughts.

5. Close your eyes if you like, keeping the eyes relaxed and lifting the level of your gaze to just above the horizon line. This eye position quiets the primitive brain, quiets the thoughts and focuses your awareness on the frontal lobes or higher consciousness part of the brain. It also helps you to stay awake while meditating.

6. Be very gentle with yourself. When you notice your mind wandering, bring your awareness back to your breath. (Notice that I said "when," not "if." It does happen, even to experienced meditators). See if you can feel the beginning and end of this breath. You may notice a pause between the in breath and the out breath; relax your attention as the breath returns naturally. Know that the breath is a wonderful place to focus our attention—because it is so accessible and available to us. Whether you are new to meditation or have practiced for a while, this technique will support

you in bringing mindfulness—relaxed, open and spacious awareness—to your meditations.

7. If you start to feel sleepy, sit up a little bit, or open your eyes—take a few deep breaths and allow the breath to become natural again. Thoughts, distractions, sensations will continue—it doesn't matter—simply come back to the breath again and again.

8. Complete your meditation with a few minutes of silent contemplation and gratitude, gently opening your eyes. See if you can bring this quality of presence and connection into your day.

DEVELOPING A
MEDITATION ROUTINE

*J*t is vital to understand that meditation is a daily
practice.

The best way to establish and integrate meditation into your
life is to have a steady routine.

When I first began meditating, I would meditate one day,
then skip a day or so, then fit it into my schedule to meditate
again. Then one day I heard—actually heard—the words
that had been said so often before, words I had read fre-
quently: Daily practice. And I got it—meditation is a daily
practice. This means it is something that you make a part of
your life on a daily basis. Every day.

1. It is very helpful to meditate at the same time every
    day, if possible.

2. Create a special place to meditate that feels safe, com-
    fortable and sacred to you.

3. You might want to bring a candle, photos, music and/
    or other sacred objects to your meditation space.

4. Request that your family honor your quiet time; you
    can invite them to join you.

5. Centering Breath—Sit comfortably, close your eyes if you like, and simply observe the breath rising and falling in the body—you might feel the breath open and soften around your heart.

6. Rest Down and Come Into Alignment—Sit comfortably—allowing your body to be supported, feel your connection to the earth for a few breaths. Rock gently side to side then forward and back, finding where you feel in balance and at ease in your body, with your spine long and open.

7. Before you end your meditation, spend some time in silent contemplation. Open to Inner Wisdom and Intuition.

8. Remember Gratitude—Express your gratitude for your guidance, for your health, home, family, friends, work—for all of the blessings in your life. Allow the gratitude to fill your being.

9. Come out of meditation gradually—noticing the transition from internal focus to external focus.

CREATING AN ENVIRONMENT FOR YOUR DAILY PRACTICE—A SACRED SPACE

*S*upporting yourself in your daily practice will smooth out the bumps we all encounter when we begin to establish a routine for meditation. Gathering with other like minded people can help us feel supported. Remember that the ultimate goal of a daily practice is continuous mindfulness and connection with yourself, with others and with all of life.

Many people struggle with finding the time for a daily practice. Some of the resistance is to establishing a daily practice can be relieved when you approach it as a gift you give yourself.

Begin to notice all of the things you already do each day. Bring mindfulness to brushing your teeth, making the bed, or preparing food. You might begin with the Preparation for Meditation instructions and sit in stillness for one minute each day, until you begin to feel comfortable and familiar with your inner world.

Creating a Sacred Space

Choosing a special place to meditate in your home or office helps to create a sacred space. It does not have to be elaborate—a comfortable chair or cushion where you feel safe, photos of family or others who inspire you, flowers, a candle or objects from nature can all add to this environment. Beautiful music can accompany you—flute, harp or other soothing instrumental music can invite you to relax and turn within.

Reading a daily meditation or affirmation can focus your meditation and time of contemplation. Most importantly—be gentle with yourself and allow yourself to change your practice until you find a routine and the environment that feels most comfortable to you.

Complete your meditation with silent contemplation and gratitude.

BRINGING MEDITATION
INTO EVERYDAY LIFE

*M*any of us feel that Meditation is something we practice once a day, or maybe twice—morning and evening. The rest of the time we get on with our lives without any thought of our spiritual practice. Once you have been meditating for some time, you might find it helpful to integrate the awareness and alignment you experience in meditation into your life more fully.

Here are some suggestions to play with:

- Practice continuous observation, without judgment. Stay connected to yourself as an expression of aliveness.

- Continuous awareness of the breath. When you feel pulled off of your center, stop and take a few slow, deep breaths. Bring to mind how calm and centered you feel in your morning meditation practice.

- See how often you can bring your attention to the spiritual eye, at the point between the eyebrows. Gently touch or tap your finger on that point with your eyes closed to bring your attention back to the present moment.

- Playfully find a moment or two throughout the day to drop into your center, perhaps when you stop at a red light, before you pick up the phone or in the bathroom. Take a slow deep breath and smile.

- Notice your inner critical voice. Give that voice the job of noticing how well things are going, rather than keeping track of all the things that aren't getting done.

- Be gentle with yourself. When you miss the mark, observe your response and give yourself credit for observing, and for the things that went well, and try again.

- Hum or chant throughout the day. The sound and vibration is healing to the body and gives your mind something to focus on. Find a sacred mantra or repeated phrase to practice that feels uplifting to you.

- Focus on being of service in all that you do. Do your best and let go of the outcome.

- Do your best to stay neutral, kind, compassionate and thoughtful in your responses to people and circumstances.

- Pray for others, especially those who challenge you. Bless and release them when necessary.

- Ask for healing light to flow through you, around you and as you.

- Try something new each day. Be creative, do everyday tasks with a fresh perspective.

- Practice with a meditation group or attend a class. Surround yourself with people who are dedicated to mindfulness and loving service.

- Create an environment that is uplifting, in your home, car and office. Beautiful images, objects, plants, flowers and music that is inspiring to you.

- Study inspiring books, CDs and programs. Attend retreats and lessons with teachers who embody the principles you would like to learn.

- Practice Energization Exercises, yoga postures and relaxation techniques to stay fit, strong and relaxed. (See Part Two)

- Remember you are a spiritual being having a human experience, rather than a human being having a spiritual experience.

- Choose to live with joy and appreciation for life.

- Embrace your challenges, learn from them, allow yourself to change and grow.

- Get out into nature as much as possible. Appreciate the abundance of Mother Nature.

- Give yourself periods of silence, calm, introspection and peacefulness.

- Bring the peace and joy of your daily meditation out into daily activities. Your success in meditation can often be measured by how happy and joyful you are in the world.

GRATITUDE MEDITATION

*A*lthough meditation alone has unquestioned benefits, including gratitude in your meditation can give you benefits beyond just the meditation itself.

- Take a few moments to relax and allow the details and pressures of the day to drift away.

- Find a quiet place to settle down and get in touch with your breath.

- Gently close your eyes and allow your awareness to settle into your body, observing the sensations of the breath.

- Connect with Mother Earth and relax into the support beneath your body. Open to your source and inner guidance.

- Bring your awareness to your heart and connect with something you are grateful for. Invite that gratitude to fill your heart with a warm glow.

- Now find something else you are grateful for.

- Continue as long as you feel comfortable and happy.

- Complete your meditation by expanding the warm glow in your heart out in all directions and send a blessing to your loved ones.

- Slowly deepen your breath, yawn, stretch and open your eyes.

- Enjoy this glow and peace of mind throughout the rest of your day.

*My soul floats
on waves of cosmic light.*

FORGIVENESS MEDITATION

So much of the benefit of healing meditation practice is about staying fully in the present moment. One of the greatest challenges to staying in the present moment is how much we continue to hold onto the past. Practicing forgiveness in the safety of your own heart is one way to release past hurt, whether related to another person, a circumstance or organization or to your own behavior. We are tied to the past as long as we continue to tell the story about what went wrong—what happened or didn't happen. We all know the yukky place of resentment, regret and sadness.

As you move through your day today, notice how much of your attention is focused on the past.

- What have you been doing or feeling that you would like to change?

- Where are you judging yourself?

- What have you done that you keep holding as unforgivable?

Gently take what you are noticing into your meditation practice, telling the truth about your feelings and ask for the willingness to release and begin to let go of the past and open up to a new way of being—gently—lovingly—gradually.

Simple Healing Meditation to Release the Past

1. Settle yourself down following some stretching and full, deep breaths.

2. Bring to mind a habit or behavior you would like to release or heal.

3. Notice in your body and thoughts how and where you are holding this story.

4. Take several slow deep breaths, allowing your heart to open and soften, relaxing and expanding into your natural goodness, compassion and unconditional love.

5. Continue to breathe, relaxing more and more in the presence of this issue, allowing the process to unfold within your consciousness, asking for higher wisdom to be revealed to you.

6. Give thanks for your willingness and courage to heal, release anger, resentment, pain and suffering for yourself and others.

Continue to practice regularly with compassion—especially for yourself, as you create space within and without for healing right here and right now. The more you are willing to practice keeping your awareness in the present moment, the easier it will become to let go of the past and stop reliving it.

WALKING
ANOTHER METHOD OF MEDITATION

*T*here are an infinite number of methods and techniques of meditation. The best one for you is the one you will feel most comfortable and willing to practice consistently.

Be gentle with yourself, especially when you are beginning to learn and practice. When you see obstacles creep in, just observe them, but don't feel that this means you're not meditating; don't get harsh or judgmental with yourself. Continue to go back to your meditation each time. The idea is to give yourself time to see which meditation practice is the one you feel you will be able to stick with, and which will serve you best.

Walking Meditation

I believe that the best way to learn this practice is to be led through it.

Standing

To begin this period of walking meditation, first of all simply stand. Stand on the spot, noticing your connection to the earth, being aware of all of the subtle movements that go on in order to keep us balanced and upright. Very often we take our ability to be able to stand upright for granted, but actually, it took us a couple of years to learn how to do this. You might gently rock side to side, noticing when you feel your weight balanced on both feet. Then rock gently forward and back, noticing when you feel centered front to back. Lengthen your spine and bring the earth energy up through your body.

Walking
Then you can begin to walk at a fairly slow but normal walking pace, and in a normal manner. Simply be aware of your body, as you begin to move.

Awareness of your body
Bring your attention to the soles of your feet, being aware of the alternating patterns of contract and release; be aware of your foot as the heel touches the ground, as your foot rolls forward onto the ball, and then lifts and moves through the air. Be aware of all the different sensations in your feet, the feeling of the inside of your shoes, the fabric of your socks, and let your feet be as relaxed as you can. Become aware of your ankles. Notice the qualities of the sensations in those joints—as each foot is on the ground, and as it then travels through the air.

Let your ankle joints be relaxed—make sure you're not holding on in any way. You can become aware of your lower legs—your shins, your calves. You can be aware of the contact with your clothing: be aware of the temperature on your skin; you can be aware of the muscles. Notice what the calf muscles are doing as you're walking. You might even want to exaggerate for a few steps what the calf muscles are doing—just so that you can connect with that—and then let your walking go back to a normal relaxed rhythm. Allow your calf muscles to be relaxed.

Then notice the sensations in your knees. Expand your awareness into your thighs. Being aware of the skin, again the contact with your clothing, the temperature. Be aware of the muscles, and notice what the muscles on the fronts of the thighs, and the muscles on the backs of the thighs are doing. And once more you might want, for a few steps, to exaggerate what those muscles are doing, and then let your walk go back to a normal rhythm.

Become aware of your hips and the muscles around your hip joints, and relax those muscles. Really relax. Even when you think you've relaxed—relax some more. Notice how that changes your stride and your pace. Notice how the rhythm and the gait of your walk change as your hips relax. You can be aware of the whole of your pelvis—and notice all of the movements that are going on in your pelvis. One hip moves forward and then the other; one hip lifting, the other sinking.

Feel your spine extending upwards—the lumbar spine, the thoracic spine—notice how it moves along with the pelvis. Your spine is in constant motion. It's swaying from side to side. There is a twisting motion around the central axis. Your spine is in constant motion.

Notice your belly; you might feel your clothing in contact with your belly, and notice how your belly is the center of your body. Very often it feels like it's "down there" because we are so much in our heads. Feel your abdomen in the center of your body, as the center of your being. Notice your chest, and just let your breathing happen. Notice the contact that your chest makes with your clothing. Noticing your shoulders, how they are moving with the rhythm of your walking. Let your shoulders be relaxed, and let your shoulders passively transmit the rhythm of your walk down into your arms. Allow your arms to swing naturally. Notice all the motions in your arms—your upper arms, your elbows, your forearms, your wrists, your hands and fingers. Feel the air moving over the skin on your hands and fingers as your arms swing through the air.

Become aware of your neck and the muscles supporting your skull. Notice the angle of your head. Also notice that as you relax the muscles on the back of your neck, your chin slightly tucks in and your head comes to a place of balance. Play around with the angle of your head and see how it changes your experience. When you lift your chin, you might notice that your experience becomes much lighter, that you become more aware of the outside world, or much more aware of your thoughts and caught up in your thoughts. And then, bring your head back to a point of balance, your chin slightly tucked in.

Relax your jaw. Relax your eyes and just let your eyes be soft, gently looking ahead, not staring at anything, not allowing yourself to be caught up in anything that's going past you.

Feelings

You can be aware of the feelings that you're having, not in terms of emotions here, but just the feeling tone. Are there things that feel pleasant; are there things that feel unpleasant whether in your body or outside of your body? When you notice things in your body that are pleasant or unpleasant, just notice them. Neither cling onto them, nor push them away, but just notice them. If you notice things in the outside world that are either pleasant or unpleasant, just allow them to drift by, allowing them to drift by without following them or moving away from them.

Thoughts and Emotions

You can notice your emotional states. Are you bored? content? irritated? Are you feeling very happy to be doing what you're doing? Again, just notice what emotions are present. Notice your mind also. Is your mind clear, or dull? Is your mind busy, or calm? Are you thinking about things unconnected with this practice, or do the thoughts that occur center on what you're doing right now. Notice these things with no particular judgment—just be aware of them.

Balancing Inner and Outer

You can notice the balance between your experience of the inner and the outer. I often find that if I can be aware of both the inner world and the outer world in equal balance, then my mind settles at a point of stillness, calmness, and clarity.

See if you can find that point of balance where you're equally aware of the inner and the outer, and your mind is calm, content, and quiet.

Stopping

Allow yourself to come to a slow and gradual stop. Do that; come to a stop. Experience yourself standing. Just notice what it's like to no longer be in motion. Notice once more the complex balancing act that's going on to keep you upright. Feel once again the weight traveling down through the soles of your feet into the earth; simply stand, and experience yourself, and, finally, bring this meditation session to a close.

In Part Two of this book we will look at a second aspect of walking meditation.

There are other methods of meditation, which you can explore later, after you have become established to some degree in a daily practice. Some of these other methods will be covered in the second part of this book. Explore these methods with curiosity, openness and willingness to learn. You will be rewarded with relaxation, clarity, connection to yourself and others, and a growing peace of mind and heart.

Namaste, which means "the light in me honors the light in you".

PART TWO

DEEPENING YOUR PRACTICE

*S*o, you've begun a meditation practice and tested the waters. After you have been enjoying a meditation practice for some time, you may be ready, even eager, to try new or different techniques, or to enhance the ones you are already using. Broadening your base of techniques will keep your practice satisfying, and increase its effectiveness. This is what is known as "deepening" your practice.

Here are a few simple options to consider:

- Adding a little time to your daily meditation. This can have some heartening results as you allow yourself to settle even more into the stillness.

- If you have been meditating in the morning for some time, you might add an evening meditation before bedtime. This can be a time of relaxation, releasing the day, giving thanks for all of the good in your life and calming your mind for a restful sleep. You might also ask to receive guidance and clarity during the night.

- Perhaps, if you have been using the breath as a point of focus, you may want to add Mantra, or a repeated phrase, (see section on Mantra) as a way to enjoy the healing benefits of sound and vibration. Choosing a mantra, such as "Hong Sau" offers a way to focus the mind as well. It also allows you to dip into the collective energy of all of the meditators and master teachers who have practiced the mantra for many years. This is one of the many wonders of meditation.

SOME ADDITIONAL
METHODS OF MEDITATION

"When you are inspired to some great purpose, some extraordinary project, all your thoughts break their bonds; your mind transcends limitations, your consciousness expands in every direction, and you find yourself in a new, great and wonderful world. Dormant forces, faculties and talents become alive, and you discover yourself to be a greater person by far than you ever dreamed yourself to be."

Patanjali—The Yoga Sutras

This quote inspires me because it describes what is possible when we practice turning within for inspiration and guidance, rather than looking outside for direction. There is a place within us that always knows what is best for us. The practice of meditation gives us access to an unlimited inner source of peace, harmony, wisdom and clarity. Meditation connects us to our inner truth. We have access to an expanded capacity for creativity, inspiration and productivity.

Over time you will become familiar with that inner source, and how it speaks to you and guides you. You may receive words or phrases, images or feelings. Be very gentle with yourself—observe the wandering mind—repeat the question and remain open and receptive. May you be rewarded with a release of anxiety, worry, doubt, fear and concern for the future.

In part one, we covered some of the more basic aspects of meditation. This section will cover some additional methods, which may also appeal to you, and which will help you to broaden the scope of your meditation.

Mentioned in Part One were:

- Mindfulness

- Focusing on the breath

- Walking Meditation—Part One

Following are some other methods you can include in your meditation practice. Continuing to explore these different methods with curiosity, openness and willingness to learn will reap gratifying rewards.

CHANTING

*A*ccording to the ancient teachings of India, of all musical instruments the most perfect is the human voice.

Sound, through the medium of the voice, is the channel through which human consciousness flows into outward manifestation. Sound has power.

Attunement—attuning ourselves to higher consciousness by repeating a chant, more and more deeply, day after day, will spiritualize the chant and take it deeper and deeper into oneself to achieve divine contact.

Om or AUM?

AUM is the highest chant, attuned to the very essence of all vibrations, the cosmic vibration itself. In English it is usually written Om. It is spiritually more correct to spell AUM, as each letter signifies a different phase of the cosmic vibration: creation, preservation, and dissolution.

Aum Namah Shivaya is another well known phrase used for chanting.

Kirtan—This is a delightful gathering of musicians and singers, chanting together.

Mantra is a form of devotional practice, a recollection of the Divine or source within all of us, to bolster our dedication to daily practice and devotion. Many simply feel a sense of comfort from chanting. Rhythmic chanting or even singing is known to stimulate the release of endorphins, which may account for the feeling of wellbeing, and even ecstasy, which accompanies group chanting. A similar effect can be enjoyed in many religious and cultural groups.

WALKING MEDITATION
PART TWO

*O*ne of my very favorite ways to practice walking meditation is to "walk the labyrinth." The labyrinth is an ancient spiritual tool in the form of a circle with a meandering, purposeful path that becomes a deep and profound metaphor for our lives.

I was introduced to the labyrinth by Dr. Lauren Artess at Grace Cathedral in San Francisco. I have found that walking this sacred path slows me down like nothing else. I really land in my body and connect to Mother Earth. The labyrinth is not a maze, it has only one path to the center and back out on the same path to the edge.

"The labyrinth is a spiritual tool meant to awaken us to the deep rhythm that unites us to ourselves and to the Light that calls from within. In surrendering to the winding path, the soul finds healing and wholeness."

Dr. Lauren Artress, author of *Walking A Sacred Path*

One way to walk the labyrinth is to set an intention or ask a question before entering. Then walk in slowly and mindfully, releasing anything that is holding you back in life.

Pause in the center of the labyrinth to pray or contemplate, then walk slowly back out, opening to guidance and clarity.

Once you become interested in the labyrinth, as I have, you will find them all over the world—in churches, gardens, retreat centers and hospitals. I invite you to explore this magical gift—walking, dancing, singing, praying, meditating—alone or with others.

HONG SAU
THE HONG SAU MANTRA FOR CONCENTRATION

This is the basic technique of meditation taught by Paramhansa Yogananda. It is a technique of concentration; when done deeply it leads naturally to a deep state of true meditation. Hong Sau mean "I am Spirit".

Preparation: Relaxation—Yoga postures are wonderful to get the energy flowing and soothe the body for easier sitting. Or use any other gentle exercises of your choice, which calm, rather than excite, the nervous system.

Prayer: Begin with a prayer. Always ask for guidance and support. Say a prayer mentally or aloud to whatever form of the Divine feels comfortable to you. Say it in the language of your own heart. Feel that you are really making contact and reaffirm your commitment. Feel and express gratitude to the Divine for all you have received, including the liberating techniques of meditation.

Chanting: If you don't play a musical instrument, sing along with a chanting tape, either aloud or mentally. Chanting opens the heart, an important ingredient for deep meditation.

Posture: Sit up straight, with your back away from the back of the chair. Place your hands, palms up on the thighs. Keep your chest open and your chin level.

Eyes: With eyelids closed, turn your eyes slightly upward as if looking at a mountain in the distance. This upward gaze should not involve any strain.

Tense and Relax: Inhale and hold your breath, tensing the entire body; then throw the breath out and relax. Do this three times.

Measured Breathing (also called Even-Count Breathing): Inhale through the nose to a count that's comfortable for you; hold your breath that same count; exhale through the nose to the same count. Begin your next inhalation immediately. Do at least six rounds, making your count as long as you can comfortably. Finish your preparation by inhaling normally, then exhaling slowly and completely. Now you are ready to practice the Hong Sau technique.

Concentration—The Hong Sau Technique

Watch the breath: Breathe through the nose, letting the breath flow as it wishes, without controlling it. Notice the breath wherever you feel it. When you begin, you may be most aware of the movement of the lungs, so watch the breath there. As your breath calms down, watch the more subtle movement of air in the nose. Eventually, watching the breath will calm your mind and lead you to concentration at the spiritual eye—the point between the eyebrows. Remember to relax and let the breath do whatever it wants and simply observe.

Repeat Hong Sau: As the breath flows in, accompany the inhalation with a mental repetition of the sound "Hong"; as the breath flows out, mentally repeat "Sau." Let the natural flow of the breath itself dictate the pace. You will notice that your breathing will naturally become more and more soft and subtle. This is perfectly normal—you may also eventually notice long pauses between breaths. Relax—your body knows how to breathe.

Ending your practice of Hong Sau: Practice for the first two-thirds to three-quarters of your meditation time. End your practice by exhaling gently three times in quick succession, then let your breath stay out as long as it comfortable, enjoying the sensation of stillness. Settle into a brief period of opening to Divine guidance—asking a specific question and listening for the answer or simply asking "What is it I need to know or understand?" Remain open and receptive to whatever comes or doesn't come. Giving thanks to your guidance and know that more will be revealed.

YOGA
ANANDA YOGA FOR HIGHER AWARENESS

The word Yoga means yoke or union. There are a number of schools of yoga offering spiritual disciplines leading to oneness with the Self, with the object being the union with the Absolute as an inner experience.

Most of us may have experienced yoga classes with various teachers who all have different training and experience. Some classes are taught simply as a physical practice and some can include spiritual practices such as pranayama (or breathing practices), chanting, deep relaxation and meditation.

I have been taught that Hatha yoga postures, or asanas, have been designed as preparation for meditation. There are a wide range of yoga postures from gentle to very advanced. I encourage you to visit various classes and speak with the instructors to find a class that is most beneficial for you and your individual body.

Yoga is an ancient practice known all over the world and can be a powerful discipline for strength, flexibility, balance and to gently massage the internal organs and eliminate waste and tension that blocks the natural flow of energy in the body.

Full Yogic Breath—This is a great place to begin your yoga practice. Stand with your feet about hip width apart and your knees soft. Exhale fully while bending forward, allowing the arms to hang and relaxing the back of your neck. When you are ready to inhale, sweep the hands up and out, fully expanding the abdomen, diaphragm and upper chest. Continue breathing and moving, listening to your body and finding your own pace. Follow your breath for several rounds.

Standing Mountain Pose—I love to teach this posture, because it doesn't look like much and there is a great deal of benefit and power in this pose. You might practice any time you are standing in line. Stand with your feet hip-width apart, knees soft, arms relaxed at your sides. Continue the Full Yogic Breath, expanding the abdomen, diaphragm and upper chest on the inhalation and fully emptying the lungs when you exhale. Lengthen your spine, drawing the energy up toward the brain. Shift your weight gently from side to side and notice when your weight is evenly distributed on both feet. Then gently shift your weight forward and back, noticing when you feel centered front to back. Now imagine that you are breathing the earth energy up through your body, opening up the flow of energy.

Child's Pose—This is a resting pose down on the floor or mat. Sit on your heels and rest your forehead on your folded hands or on the floor in front of your knees, with your arms down at your sides. Turn your attention inward and allow your body to relax as much as possible. The affirmation is: *"I relax into my inner haven of peace."*

Savasana or Corpse Pose—Lie flat on your back on your yoga mat or a blanket, with your arms and legs in a comfortable position. You may find that a bolster or blanket rolled up under your knees and a towel rolled up under your neck will help with finding a comfortable position.

Lie in this pose for at least five to ten minutes following yoga postures. It is very beneficial to balance the movement with stillness, allowing your body to activate the relaxation response. The affirmation is: "*Bones, muscles, movement. I surrender now; anxiety, elation and depression, churning thoughts. All these I give into the hands of peace.*"

The highest goal of yoga practice is to reach a state of ease, where it is no longer necessary to engage in formal practice, but to remain in a state of divine union while going about daily activities.

I encourage you to explore yoga practice to improve your health and fitness as well as to bring ease and calm to your life. After all, when the great yoga master Yogananda was asked by his students about the best yoga posture, he was heard to say, "Standing on your own two feet!"

ENERGIZATION EXERCISES

*E*nergization exercises are a gift from Paramahansa Yogananda as preparation for yoga and meditation practice. There is a complete system of 39 exercises which increases the flow of life-force to strengthen and energize your entire body. Through direct experience they help to clear and focus the mind, and assist in deepening our understanding of our true nature as pure energy.

I first experienced these exercises many years ago on my first visit to the Expanding Light at Ananda in Nevada City, California, and now practice them every morning. Even when I'm sore and achy, when I am able to get up and do these simple exercises, I immediately feel better, clearer, looser, and more motivated to exercise and begin my day.

There are 39 double breath—tense and release exercises that move throughout the body, increasing respiration and circulation and warming up the body, while lifting the energy up toward the brain.

At the Expanding Light, the Energization Exercises are taught at dawn and every afternoon, right before yoga postures and meditation sessions. Greeting the rising sun with breathing, stretching and affirmations is simply glorious!

Here is a description of the exercises. They really need to be experienced to appreciate their full effect:

1. Double Breath Inhalation/Exhalation. We begin with two short, sharp inhalations through the nose, long, strong inhalations—completely filling the lungs. Then, exhale through your nose and mouth, first with a short exhalation, then a long exhalation to empty the lungs completely.

2. Keep your awareness on the flow of energy throughout your body, focusing on the medulla oblongata at the base of the brain. Just as we consume food through our mouths, prana (or life-force energy) enters the body through the medulla.

3. As you alternately tense and release various body parts, you are directing energy with your concentration to recharge the body with energy and train the brain to bring the flow of prana under your conscious control.

4. Tense each body part—low—medium—high—in a smooth progression, hold for 2 to 3 seconds, then relax—high—medium—low, until completely relaxed. Concentrate deeply on the center of each muscle or muscle group and notice and feel the result as you gradually increase and decrease tension.

5. Keep an attitude of openness, expansion and cooperation as you draw and direct the limitless stream of energy. Tense with will, relax and feel.

6. Be very gentle with yourself. When you feel fatigued or injured, use low tension and direct the energy mentally while you visualize healing light flowing into your body part.

7. You might begin your practice with a prayer. I use: "Oh Infinite Spirit! Recharge my body with conscious cosmic energy. Recharge my mind with concentration and determination. Recharge my soul and all souls with ever new Joy. Oh eternal youth of body and mind, abide within me forever and ever. Om, peace, amen."

If there is another prayer or invocation you feel comfortable with, you can use that.

ENERGIZATION EXERCISES
SHORT VERSION

Sometimes the full set of 39 Energization exercises takes more time than you have available. Here is an abbreviated version with very good benefits. These exercises can be practiced by anyone of any age or level of ability, standing, seated or lying down. I've even heard it is beneficial to practice or even visualize the exercises when bed-ridden.

1. Double breathing, palms touching: double inhale, tensing the body up from the feet, with arms opening out to the sides. Double exhale, relaxing downward, bringing the arms together out in front, knees flexed, feeling the energy between the hands. Repeat this 3–5 times.

2. Hands-on-shoulders rotation: Place hands on shoulders, with elbows down, rotate the entire shoulder joint three times forward and three times back.

3. Spinal rotation: Separate your feet a bit more than hip width apart, lean slightly and gently forward and stabilize hips and pelvis. Keeping the spine straight and lower body stable, begin to make circles with the upper body, three times in each direction.

4. Upper body rotation: With arms straight ahead at shoulder height, keep hips stationary and swing to the left, left arm behind you, right fist to the chest, with the head following the movement of the left arm. Tense the upper back, not the arms. Repeat to the right side, three times on each side.

5. Skull tapping: With the fingertips of both hands, tap all over the scalp to increase the circulation and improve the memory.

6. Scalp massage: With the fingertips, rub briskly all over the scalp, moving the scalp around on the skull, not just moving the hair around.

7. 20-part body recharging:

   a. Double inhale, tense your whole body and hold the tension. Then double exhale.

   b. Tense 20 individual body parts: left foot, right foot, left calf, right calf, left buttock, right buttock, lower abdomen, stomach above navel, left forearm, right forearm, left upper arm, right upper arm, left neck, right neck, front of neck, back of neck.

   c. Tense upward adding one body part at a time as you inhale slowly. When you reach the top, vibrate with everything tensed. Exhale slowly, relaxing all body parts, then the other body parts in reverse order.

8. Whole-body breathing: Exhale. Bend over from the hips, relax your entire body, especially the arms, neck and back. Double inhale as you sweep your hands, palms inward, up the front of your body and over your head, lifting the energy. Relax forward, sweeping the hands down toward the feet and relax completely as you exhale. Do this three times. (This can be practiced by itself at any time for vitalizing energy.)

WHAT IS VISIONING
GUIDED MEDITATION?

"It is our purpose and destiny to bring a new dimension into this world by living in conscious oneness with the totality and conscious alignment with universal intelligence."

Eckhart Tolle—*A New Earth*

*V*isioning is a meditation practice which allows us to access our inner wisdom and come into alignment with universal intelligence. You allow the vision to unfold in your consciousness and watch how your dreams manifest in your every day life. Be patient with the process, remembering to let go of thinking and trying to figure out what to DO!

Open, open, open...

You may Vision for a specific topic, such as health or career, or you may ask an open ended question and listen with your heart for the answers. (For example: What is it I need to know or understand?) Your guidance may come in the form of words or phrases, images or feelings. Be patient with yourself as you practice and develop attuning to your intuition, taking action from a place of clarity, willingness and inspiration. This takes some practice to attune yourself to listening within for guidance.

The Visioning Questions:

1. What is Spirit's vision (or the Highest vision) for my life? What is the vision for my health and well-being?

2. What am I releasing or forgiving to fulfill this vision—what am I releasing that no longer serves me?

3. What am I embracing or welcoming into my experience?

4. What must I BE for this vision to be fulfilled—what qualities will support me as I grow and learn?

You might want to set aside extra time following your meditation to write about your experience. Often more information and clarity is gained as we are writing. You might ask for guidance about how to take inspired action—staying in touch with the feelings that are being revealed. Also, stay open to the demonstrations and fulfillment of your vision over subsequent days and weeks. You will be amazed at the results as you come into alignment with your vision.

CHAKRAS
UNDERSTANDING YOUR ENERGY BODY

The chakras are energy centers, or gateways located within the inner, astral spine. It is said that there is a sound made by each chakra, which can be heard in deep, silent meditation. Listen especially in your right ear. When you hear one of the sounds of the chakras, allow yourself to be absorbed into it. When you hear the sound of Om (also spelled Aum), forget all other sounds or techniques and concentrate on this sound—let it absorb you into itself.

"Aum is the bridge between human consciousness and cosmic consciousness."

Paramahansa Yogananda

Each chakra has a name, and is placed in a specific area in relation to the physical body. Here are the chakras, in order moving up from the bottom of the spine:

First or Root Chakra

Location: Base of the spine.
Element: Earth
Color: Red
Spiritual Connection: Tribal Power
Sound: Bumblebee Note: G below middle C
When you are in harmony with the First Chakra: Profound connection to nature. A deep understanding of nature's ebb and flow.
When you are out of harmony: Inability to trust. Focus on survival. Needing to satisfy own needs and desires.

Second or Sacral Chakra

Location: Lower abdomen above genitals.
Element: Water
Color: Orange
Spiritual Connection: Relationships
Sound: Flute or tinkling stream Note: A
In harmony: Happy connection to life, open, happy, kind and willing to engage with others.
Out of harmony: Unsure, unstable in relationships. Restrained emotionally, suppressing natural needs.

Third or Lumbar Chakra

Location: Stomach or solar plexus.
Element: Fire
Color: Yellow
Spiritual Connection: Personal Power
Sound: Harp Note: B-flat
In harmony: Wholeness, inner calm and peaceful feelings. Tolerance and acceptance of others. Balance of material and spiritual world.
Out of harmony: Distrust of the natural flow of life. Need to dominate others. Great need for material security.

Fourth or Heart Chakra

Location: Center of chest.
Element: Air
Color: Green
Spiritual Connection: Emotional Power
Sound: Gong or bells Note: D
In harmony: Acceptance and understanding of life and relationships. Feelings of wholeness and harmony. Balance of inner and outer life.
Out of harmony: Unable to give and receive love. Insincere in relationships.

Fifth or Throat Chakra

Location: Between collarbones.

Element: Ether

Color: Light Blue

Spiritual Connection: Power of Will

Sound: Wind in trees Note: E-flat

In harmony: Balance of self-expression, silence and speech. Trusting of intuition. Able to speak one's truth.

Out of harmony: Much talking without true self-expression. Fear of being judged. Afraid of silence.

Sixth or Spiritual Chakra

Location: Between the eyebrows.

Element: All

Color: Indigo

Spiritual Connection: Power of Mind

Sound: Aum Note: F

In harmony: Awareness of spiritual being. Intuition and inner wisdom brought into everyday life. Connection to Divine source.

Out of harmony: Focus on mental and intellectual only. Disconnected from intuition. Seeing only obvious or surface meaning.

Seventh or Crown Chakra

Location: Top of head
Element: All
Color: Violet
Spiritual Connection: Unity Consciousness
Sound: Aum Note: G above middle C
In harmony: Living in unity with all of life. The self connects to the Divine. Release individual ego.
Out of harmony: Anxious and fearful. Depressed and unfulfilled.

CHAKRA MEDITATION

You can gain a greater awareness of the chakras by chanting the OM while focusing your attention on each chakra. You do this by visualizing energy moving through each chakra, beginning at the base of the spine and going up and down several times. End with the 6th chakra, also called the ajna center, or the spiritual eye. In this way you can remove stuck energy, blockages that can impede the natural flow of energy through the body.

REDUCING STRESS
WITH MINDFULNESS

*M*indfulness means connecting deeply and directly with what is actually happening.

We know that everything is always changing—inside and outside. Change is constant. Though many humans do not seem to like or welcome change that is not self-initiated, we all have a gift, which is the capacity—despite changes—to be kind to ourselves. We have an innate ability to feel at home in our lives, and to have a sense of happiness and contentment. We may not be aware of this capacity, but meditation practice helps us uncover it. You may want to ask yourself:

1. Do I have a regular routine of movement and breathing designed to reduce daily stress?

2. How do I approach daily nutrition, hydration, restful sleep and relaxation time?

3. Do I identify my needs, directly asking for what I want/ need from family, friends and co-workers?

4. Have I regularly scheduled time away from responsibilities for recreation and renewal?

5. How do I define play—being in nature? enjoying a dance class? reading a good book? skipping?

REMINDER
FOCUSING ON THE BREATH

*T*his section was also in Part One, as part of the basics. I include it here because, basic though it may be, it is also a continuing practice which goes deeper and deeper as your practice develops. Pay attention to the questions, and answer them with complete commitment to deepening.

1. Sit comfortably with eyes closed and observe the breath moving in and out of the body.

2. Notice any sounds you hear—listen. When your mind wanders—gently begin again.

3. Observe the quality of the breath, the feeling of the air moving through your nostrils. Continue.

This may seem like a very simple practice. It is. It is also quite profound.

- Can you stay fully present and concentrate in this moment?

- Can you fully experience this breath without judgment or tension?

- Can you release the habit of telling a story about everything as it is happening?

Be kind to yourself; cultivate happiness and contentment in this precious moment.

Strength and courage fill my body cells.

LOVINGKINDNESS

*T*he Pali or Sanskrit word for lovingkindness is metta, sometimes translated simply as "love." We often speak of love, but "lovingkindness" is a less familiar term to most of us. Typically, the word love conjures up thoughts of passion, which is associated with attachment, wanting, owning, and possessing. This is actually a state which is often accompanied by great fear and anxiety, which makes the "love" a conditional offering.

In contrast, the spirit of metta is a freely offered gift. Like water pouring from one vessel to another, it flows freely, taking the shape of each situation without changing its essence. If somebody disappoints you or fails to meet your expectations, your feeling of lovingkindness can still remain. By the same token, your lovingkindness toward yourself need not be destroyed when you feel, as we all do sometimes, that you have let yourself down.

It is said that the Buddha first taught metta meditation as an antidote to fear. According to legend, he sent a group of monks to meditate in a forest that was inhabited by tree spirits. The tree spirits resented the monks' presence, so they decided to scare them away. The monks fled the forest, begging, "Please, Lord Buddha, send us to meditate in some other forest." The Buddha said, "I'm going to send you back to the very same forest—but this time, I'll give you the only protection you need." He then taught them to recite the phrases and to do the heartfelt practice of lovingkindness. It is said that the monks returned to the forest and practiced metta. The tree spirits were so moved by the energy of lovingkindness that they decided to serve and protect the monks.

The practice of lovingkindness relies on our ability to open continuously to the truth of our actual experience, not cutting off the painful parts, and not trying to pretend things are other than they are. Our minds are open and expansive—spacious enough to contain all the pleasures and pains of a life fully lived. Pain is part of the reality of human experience and an opportunity for us to practice maintaining our authentic presence.

The Buddha taught that the mental forces that bring suffering can temporarily obstruct positive forces like love or wisdom, but they can never destroy them. Love is a greater power than fear or anger or guilt, so it has the capacity to undo painful mind states. The manifestations of our mental conditioning challenge us to see them for what they are and to remember our own true nature. We come back to our natural radiance and the purity of our minds by experiencing metta.

Loving others without any love for ourselves is not really possible, because it tramples on healthy boundaries, and leads to what is called "codependency." Lack of true self-love thwarts the search for true intimacy, because the focus is not on others, but on ourselves and the need to find love, rather than giving and sharing it.

The beginning of being able to extend true lovingkindness toward all beings everywhere comes when we contact our own true nature, and experience the natural radiance and purity of our minds and hearts. Lovingkindness is an essential requirement for experiencing the quality of love we all so deeply want to give and receive.

Benefits of Lovingkindness

You sleep well, while enjoying pleasant dreams and awaken easily. People love you and celestial beings (devas) love and protect you. You are safe from external dangers. Your face is radiant and your mind serene. You will be unconfused at the moment of death and take rebirth in the higher, happier realms.

The Phrases of Metta

Note: If these phrases do not touch your heart, come up with your own. The important thing is to use words that are meaningful to you.

May I be free from danger. May I be happy. May I be healthy. May I live with ease.

May you be free from danger. May we be free from danger.

Another version of this practice, which has been turned into a well-known chant, is:

May I be filled with lovingkindness, may I be well.

May I be peaceful and at ease and may I be happy.

May you be filled with lovingkindness...

May we be filled with lovingkindness...

The Practice of Metta: The traditional practice uses a series of phrases directed, in order, to yourself, to someone you find inspiring or to whom you feel grateful. Next, move on to a beloved friend and then on to a person you may encounter in your daily life who is neutral or you don't know well.

Now you are ready to send lovingkindness to someone with whom you have had difficulty or conflict. Doing this practice does not mean you are excusing their behavior; rather, you are engaging in the marvelous process of discovering and cultivating your inherent capacity for unconditional love. Directing metta toward a difficult person leads to the discovery of your own capacity for lovingkindness that is born of freedom.

In the final phase of the practice, we move on to offer metta to all beings everywhere, without distinction or exception.

Lovingkindness Chant

May I be filled with loving kindness, May I be well.

May I be peaceful and at ease and may I be happy.

May you be filled...

May we be filled...

Sing each verse several times begining with yourself, then direct the chant to a loved one, then to someone from whom you feel distance or difficulty, then to all beings. I like to bring the chant back into my own heart, for one more round of "May I be filled with lovingkindness..." while placing hands on heart.

MANTRA

A mantra is a word or phrase that is repeated, generally without sounding it out loud. The purpose of repeating a mantra is to keep the mind focused on the sound, rather than the myriad thoughts that randomly float through the mind, especially when one is trying to meditate. In meditation a mantra is a means of quieting and focusing the mind.

A mantra is very similar to saying the Rosary or repeating affirmations. The ritual of repeating a phrase, chant or prayer helps to quiet the mind and bring us into alignment with our higher selves. In some practice groups, a guru will initiate their students and transmit a mantra to them, which is their mantra for life. I believe that the sound and vibration of chanting or repeating a mantra is very healing and comforting to the body and the mind.

Affirmations can be considered mantras, especially if they are used repeatedly over a long period of time in the same way that a one or two word mantra is practiced.

You may approach chanting a mantra as a way to attune yourself to the Divine flow or Source. It is also possible to relax into the flow of a mantra that has been spiritualized and repeated by thousands of people over the years. Such mantras are well known, whereas personal, initiation mantras are individually given, and are not revealed to others.

I personally find that when I begin my meditation with first focusing on the breath and then repeating the Hong Sau mantra silently for several minutes, my mind quiets down to a point of stillness where my breath is very soft, gentle and my thoughts are quiet.

All of these techniques are preparation for meditation; in some practices, simply reciting mantra over and over is itself a form of meditation.

Allow time at the end of your meditation to release all techniques of observing the breath, chanting or repeating a mantra. Simply rest in the stillness with an open heart, focusing on the point between the eyebrows, which is considered the spiritual eye.

EATING MEDITATION

Recognition, Acceptance, and Healthy Detachment = Freedom

*E*ating meditation is a wonderful way to practice mind-fulness and deepen your awareness—something you do every day for your physical nourishment. If you have food issues, such as weight, diabetes, acid reflux or high blood pressure, this practice may profoundly shift your relationship with food.

1. Hold a berry or a raisin in your hand. Pretend you've never seen one before. Be curious. Take your time—how does it look? How does it feel? How does it smell?

2. Check in with your breath. Is your mouth watering yet? Are you hungry? Are you anxious? Do you really want this food?

3. Think about all of the people and elements involved in bringing this food into your hand. The growers, truckers, retailers, packagers—the soil, the sun, the rain, the wind.

4. Give thanks for your ability to hold this food, to see it, to feel it, to smell it, to appreciate the gift of nourishment. Notice the sensations in your body.

5. Now—very mindfully—bring the berry to your lips, experience it fully as you put it onto your tongue and taste it.

6. What is happening in your body now? Begin to chew it slowly. Savor it. Thoroughly chew and swallow. Do you still taste the flavor? Relax and enjoy the sensations.

Devote yourself in this way to your first bite of food (or more!) every day each time you eat, and notice how your relationship with food is enhanced by mindful appreciation. Give thanks and enjoy!

ZAPCHEN WELL-BEING
PRACTICES

*A*s my teacher, Julie Henderson, Ph.D., says in the introduction to her book—"What this book is for is to show you—rather, remind you—of the kinds of simple things we can do to feel better in ourselves—physically and emotionally—NO MATTER WHAT ELSE IS GOING ON."

Zapchen is a Tibetan word, given to Julie by her heart teacher, that pronounced one way can mean very high level practitioners, and pronounced slightly differently, can mean something very impolite!

My experience with these well-being practices have profoundly changed my life, in a good way.

1. Jiggling—Allow your whole body to jiggle, gently. Moving your arms, legs, head, internal organs and brain—lubricating joints, pumping diaphragms, moving fluids. Even more fun when you make noise as would a five year old. This causes rhythmic pulsation throughout the body.

2. Yawning—We all know how to yawn, yes? Unfortunately, we are taught to stifle our yawns, because it isn't polite. The heck with that. Yawning relaxes the jaw, neck, throat and cools and relaxes the brain. It also improves digestion, moves fluids and releases tryptophan which brightens you up during the day and helps you sleep at night.

3. Humming—Oh, this is a very important and effective practice, also fun with a partner. Hum and let the hum move through your body as vibration—feel the sound moving through your body. Notice where you feel the hum. Hum for a bit and then rest. Hum a bit more and rest. The sound is very comforting, relaxing and toning for our bodies. You may try humming into parts of your body that are tight, sore or in need of healing.

I've enjoyed teaching jiggling, yawning and humming in my yoga and meditation classes for many years. When I started attending Julie Henderson's once a month practice groups in Napa ten years ago, I wasn't able to relax enough to nap after we practiced together. Believe it or not, napping is a very important part of the practice, to integrate the learning. Ahhhh...

Attending week long retreats with Julie has offered me a deeper experience of listening to my body wisdom and truly allowing myself to relax and release the past. I feel the blessings from my beloved teacher, her love, support and understanding and the protection and love from her teachers, the Tibetan lamas, including the Dalai Lama.

I have great respect and gratitude for the lineage of Tibetan Buddhism as it is transmitted to us through Julie's somatic practices. I haven't felt guided to seek a guru as so many folks do who study yoga and meditation. I have, however, been blessed to come into the presence of wonderful teachers, both at Ananda and in Napa, who practice what they teach and bring deep and rich practices to their students. I honor them for their dedication to teaching, their love, kindness, humor and patience with me.

I have intuitively blended these well-being practices with the lineage from Yogananda through my beloved teachers at Ananda. Somehow it all makes sense to me and enhances and informs my life and my daily practice in wonderful ways.

My heart's desire is that you will try some of these practices and that they help you find healing, growth and enjoyment in your practice.

Practicing with a group of loving friends can bring warmth, company and deep acceptance. Spiritual community is important for our safety, support and comfort on the path.

If these practices are appealing to you, I encourage you to visit zapchen.com and get your hands on *Embodying Well-Being* by Julie Henderson, Ph.D. for more information.

FINAL COMMENTS
CONTINUING YOUR PRACTICE

It has been a great joy to share with you some of what I have learned and practiced with meditation over the years. Once you begin and are open to the practice, you will find a warm and open community of like-minded people and infinite resources and materials to explore.

Give yourself the gift of a few minutes of meditation each day and you will begin to appreciate all of the blessings in your life more fully.

Find a meditation group or meditate with a friend. Meditate with your partner and children, your cat or your dog. Animals and children are wonderful meditators.

I encourage your to come back again and again to this book, to some of the books I have suggested, to videos, audios and other on-line resources to support you in your practice.

You may move away from meditating at times and come back to the practice throughout your life. It is always available to you and the benefits are many.

GLOSSARY

Ananda means bliss.

Ananda Yoga—*Ananda Yoga for Higher Awareness*[1] is a system of Hatha Yoga established by Kriyananda, a disciple of Paramahansa Yogananda, and is based on his Kriya Yoga teachings. Ananda Yoga emphasizes inner awareness; energy control; and the experience of each asana as a natural expression of a higher state of consciousness, which is enhanced by the use of affirmations.

Buddha—Also known as Siddhartha Gautama, he was a sage on whose teachings Buddhism was founded. He was born in the Shakya republic in the Himalayan foothills and taught primarily in northeastern India. Buddha means "awakened one" or "the enlightened one." He taught a Middle Way between sensual indulgence and the severe asceticism or the renunciation movement common in his region.

Chanting—Chanting mantra or the name of God/Spirit is a commonly used spiritual practice. Chanting is a form of prayer for personal or group practice. Many spiritual traditions consider chanting a route to spiritual development.

Daily Practice—This is a concept that I heard about for years before it really sunk in. When you choose to develop a daily practice of yoga, meditation or other spiritual practices, they can be very helpful in your growth and healing. Dedicating this time to letting go of the outside world and reconnecting with yourself every day can be life changing. Consider setting an intention and creating a ritual for yourself. Create a safe and sacred space in your home or office. Begin with breathing practices to center yourself, get in touch with your body and quiet your mind. Perhaps you will want to relax or increase your energy. Try out some stretching, yoga postures or walk to enjoy movement with mindfulness. Include some time to journal and reflect to capture the insights you have gained in this dedicated time for yourself.

Drukchen—my teacher's teacher in Nepal, Gyalwang Drukpa, www.drukpa.org

Energization Exercises—A vital part of Ananda Yoga, are Yogananda's contribution to the science of yoga. He first developed them in 1916, within his organization then called "Yogoda," which he changed to Self-Realization Fellowship in the 1930's. He later expanded them into a set of 39 exercises. The goal is to tap into cosmic energy, recharging the whole body. Yogananda explains in his *Autobiography of a Yogi*: "Realizing that man's body is like an electric battery, I reasoned that it could be recharged with energy through the direct agency of the human will…. I therefore taught the Ranchi students my simple "Yogoda" techniques by which the life force, centered in man's medulla oblongata, can be consciously and instantly recharged from the unlimited supply of cosmic energy."

Guided Meditation—This is a form of meditation with guidance from a person's live voice or by a recording of a voice. You are invited to follow verbal instructions to relax the entire body, clear the mind, concentrate on breathing, and focus attention and awareness in the present moment. This form of meditation is very helpful when learning to meditate.

Guru—Sanskrit term for "teacher" or "master", especially in Indian traditions. In the Hindu tradition wisdom is transmitted from teacher to student.

Lineage—In the yoga tradition, lineage refers to ones teachers and their teachers.

Mala—Buddhist prayer beads are a traditional tool used to count the number of times a mantra is recited while meditating. They are similar to other forms of prayer beads used in various world religions; some call this tool the Buddhist rosary.

Mantra—Mantra means a sacred word, sound, syllable, or group of words believed to have psychological and spiritual power. The use, structure, function, importance and types of mantras vary according to the school and philosophy of Hinduism and of Buddhism. At its simplest, the word Aum or Om serves as a mantra and is effective as a way to focus the mind.

Meditation—To engage in mental exercise (as concentration on one's breathing or repetition of a mantra) for the purpose of reaching a heightened level of spiritual awareness. Meditation is also very helpful for relaxation, concentration and is said to be more restful than sleep.

Metta—Lovingkindness Meditation—Metta is loving-kindness, friendliness, benevolence, friendship, good will, kindness and active interest in other. This is love without clinging. The cultivation of loving-kindness is a popular form of meditation in Buddhism. The the Theravadin Buddhist tradition, this practice begins with the meditator cultivating loving-kindness toward themselves, then toward loved ones, friends, teachers, strangers, enemies, and finally towards all sentient beings.

Mindfulness—A spiritual or psychological practice that is of great important in the path of enlightenment. It is the seventh element of the noble eightfold path.

Obstacles or Hindrances—In Buddhism, the five hindrances are mental factors that hinder progress in meditation and in our daily lives. We all experience these obstacles, such as, 1) Seeking happiness in sight, sound, smell, taste and physical feeling. 2) Resentment, hatred or bitterness. 3) Heaviness of the body and dullness of the mind. 4) Restlessness or the mind and body. 5) Doubt or lack of trust. Hindrances may be managed through mindfulness, curiosity, loving kindness, lifting ones energy and by developing contentment.

Paramahansa Yogananda—(January 5, 1893–March 7, 1952), born Mukunda Lal Ghosh, was an Indian yogi and guru who introduced millions of westerners to the teachings of meditation and Kriya Yoga through his book, *Autobiography of a Yogi*.

Quotation: *"You are walking on the earth as in a dream. Our world is a dream within a dream; you must realize that to find God is the only goal, the only purpose, for which you are here. For Him alone you exist. Him you must find."*

From the book *Divine Romance*

Signature: *Paramhansa Yogananda*

Patanjali—The Yoga Sūtras of Patañjali are 196 Indian sutras or aphorisms that constitute the foundational text of Yoga. Although the Yoga Sutras have become the most important text of Yoga, the opinion of many scholars is that Patanjali was not the creator of Yoga, which existed well before him, but merely a great expounder.

Prana—The Sanskrit word for "life force" in yoga, oriental medicine and martial arts, the term refers to a cosmic energy believed to come from the sun and connecting the elements of the universe. The universal principle of energy or force, responsible for the body's life, heat and maintenance, prana is the sum total of all energy that is manifest in the universe. In Yoga the three main channels of prana are the Ida, the Pingala and the Sushumna. Ida relates to the right side of the brain, and the left side of the body, terminating at the left nostril. Pingala relates to the left side of the brain and right side of the body, terminating at the right nostril. Alternate nostril breathing balances the prana that flows within the body.

Pranayama—Sanskrit word meaning "extension of the prana or breath" or, "extension of the life force". The word is composed of two Sanskrit words, "prana", life force, or vital energy, particularly the breath and "ayama", to extend or draw out.

Somatics—Derived from the word "Somatic" (Greek "somatikos", soma: "living, aware, bodily person") which means, pertaining to the body, experienced and regulated from within.

Taking Refuge—This is a ritual engaged in Buddhist traditions with the teacher. Taking refuge in the Buddha or teacher; the Dharma, the teachings and in the Sangha, the community.

Vipasana—In the Buddhist tradition, vipasana means insight into the true nature of reality through mindfulness of the breath.

Yoga Postures or Asanas—In the Yoga Sutras, Patanjali suggests that yoga postures be "steady and comfortable". Yoga postures are designed as preparation for meditation and provide many benefits, such as improved flexibility, strength, circulation and balance. They may also reduce stress, anxiety, fatigue, sleep disturbances and hypertension. They improve physical health and quality of life in so many ways.

Zapchen—The practices and principles of Zapchen Somatics are a direct approach to embodying well-being, otherwise referred to as "feeling as good as you can—inspite of everything."

RESOURCES
&
MEDITATION CENTERS

Crystal Clarity Publishers: www.crystalclarity.com

ENERGIZATION EXERCISES: DVD from Crystal Clarity Publishers—The Expanding Light at the Ananda Retreat Center—teaches the Energization Exercises as shared by Swami Kriyananda, a direct disciple of Yogananda, and the founder of the Ananda communities worldwide. www.crystalclarity.org

I encourage you to get the DVD in order to experience the Energization Exercises for yourself. I personally practice these exercises daily.

The Expanding Light at Ananda, Nevada City, California: www.expandinglight.org

Gratitude Video—www.youtube.com/watch?v=oHv6vTKD6lg

Spirit Rock, Woodacre, CA: www.spiritrock.org

Sonoma Ashram, Sonoma, CA: www.sonomaashram.org

Zapchen Community, Napa, CA: www.zapchen.com

www.permissiontorelax.com

www.ingramcontent.com/pod-product-compliance
Lightning Source LLC
LaVergne TN
LVHW021401080426
835508LV00020B/2398